In My Feelings Series

V O L U M E   II

OTHER BOOKS BY ROBERT M. DRAKE

Spaceship (2012)
The Great Artist (2012)
Science (2013)
Beautiful Chaos (2014)
Beautiful Chaos 2 (2014)
Black Butterfly (2015)
A Brilliant Madness (2015)
Beautiful and Damned (2016)
Broken Flowers (2016)
Gravity: A Novel (2017)
Star Theory (2017)
Chaos Theory (2017)
Light Theory (2017)
Moon Theory (2017)
Dead Pop Art (2017)
Chasing The Gloom: A Novel (2017)
Moon Matrix (2018)
Seeds of Wrath (2018)
Dawn of Mayhem (2018)
The King is Dead (2018)
What I Feel When I Don't Want To Feel (2019)
What I Say To Myself When I Need To Calm The Fuck Down (2019)
What I Say When I'm Not Saying A Damn Thing (2019)
What I Mean When I Say Miss You, Love You & Fuck You (2019)
What I Say To Myself When I Need To Walk Away, Let Go And Fucking Move On (2019)
What I Really Mean When I Say Good-bye, Don't Go And Leave Me The Fuck Alone (2019)
The Advice I Give Others But Fail To Practice My Damn Self (2019)
The Things I Feel In My Fucking Soul And The Things That Took Years To Understand (2019)

For Excerpts and Updates please follow:

Instagram.com/rmdrk
Facebook.com/rmdrk
Twitter.com/rmdrk

ISBN: 978-1-7326901-1-0

Book Cover: Robert M. Drake

*For The Ones Who Feel Like They've Lost
Everything*

CONTENTS

THE THINGS I FEEL IN MY FUCKING SOUL AND THE THINGS THAT TOOK YEARS TO UNDERSTAND

ROBERT M. DRAKE

FREE YOURSELF

You don't have to
impress anyone

and you don't
have to

be nice
or polite

either.

You just have
to be yourself

even if it makes
them uncomfortable.

Be yourself
even if

the outcome hurts.

Not everyone
is going to like you

or be there
for you.

So why
do you feel obligated

to try
to be friends

with people
who don't

genuinely care
about you.

Why
do you feel

compelled
to apologize

for things
that are not

your fault.

You don't have to
do

none of these
things.

You just
keep your head up,

smile
and keep it moving.

I know this is cliché

but goddamnit!

Your world
should revolve

around you
and your happiness

and nothing else.

AMEN.

DON'T SEE IT COMING

You shouldn't
have to force

someone
to love you.

Let it come
naturally.

Sometimes
the best relationships

in life...

are the ones
we don't see

coming.

*The few we don't
expect.*

MORE HOPE

We have this
tendency

to ignore
the ignored.

This tendency
to forget our past—to

forget
how to attend

to ourselves.

We forget
so many things

and it's not because
of this

or that.

It's because
we are all

so caught up
in the present

that

we barely give
any thought

to our past—to
our future.

Everything is sadness.
Everything is stress.

Everything is debt.

Everything in the *now*
is shoved down our throats

to the point
that we can't

make room for anything
that matters.

For things
we once looked forward to

or spent
our time on.

We have forgotten
how to live,

what to live for
and why.

We have forgotten
what's important to us.

We have forgotten
the well-being

of other people.

It's hard to see
others empowering others.

It's hard to see
others wanting others

to succeed.

It's rare to see people
really care.

Really feel things
with their souls

and change.

We have so much
to look forward to

but it is hard

to indulge in these things
when everything

I need
to survive

keeps bringing me down...
keeps

blinding me
to what's really

in my heart.

We need less pain.

Less suffering.
Less stress.

Less debt.
Less agony.

Less systematic platforms
designed to bring us down.

We need less war
and more love.

More friendship—comradeship.

We need more understanding.

More hope.
More respect.

More rest.
More humanity...

but it's brutal out there,

that
I know

and it's hard
to abide by these things.

It's hard
to follow your childhood

dreams—to
remember

what your life was
before the responsibilities.

But this,
I urge of you.

This
I want for you,

all of you.

Find victory
in tragedy.

Find light
in darkness.

Find laughter
in tears.

Find joy
in stress.

And find love
in hatred.

Everything is connected.
Everything is balanced.

You just have to
pay attention

and stop ignoring
the solutions when they

are presented
to you

right before your eyes.

So it may be
a good thing

or even a bad thing.

But it is up to you
to find the goodness

in all things.

It is up to you
to not let things

terrible things
that press you down

affect you.

Life can be beautiful
but only

if you let it be.

And only
if you pay attention

to all the things
you deserve.

MAYBE LOVE

Maybe love
isn't what we've been

told.

Maybe it's not
all romance

and not
all attraction.

Maybe love is a friend.

Someone
who understands you.

Someone
who wants what's best

for you
and prays for you

especially
when you're at

your worst.

SET IT

If they love you
they won't control you.

They'll take
the chaos

in your heart
and set it free.

IT IS COMING

That same storm
that will break you

will also
make you.

And you can either
lose focus

or learn from it.

The choice is yours
and if you can't

recognize the blessing
in that.

Then you have a lot
of soul searching

to do.

The choice
is always yours

and how you let things
affect you

is ultimately
up to you.

Change is coming.
A storm is coming.

The rain is coming.

Just don't forget
to pack

your umbrella.

NOISE

You have so many
people

who love you—too
many opportunities

to grow from
and a long list

of places
you've seen.

It's a beautiful life,

yes,
indeed it is.

But place yourself within.

Listen to yourself.
Pay attention to yourself.

Are you happy
with who you are?

Are you okay
with all the decisions

you've made?

With all the people
you've had to let go?

Are you completely
in love

with who you are?

With whom
you can become?

Sure there's money.
There's fame.

There are so many things
you can buy

but here's the secret
not many

know of.

All of those things
will mean nothing...

if you're not happy
with yourself.

All those things

will soon become
forgotten victories...

if you're not
real with yourself.

You have goals,
of course,

we all do

but what good
are these goals

if you don't
love yourself.

If you don't
accept your flaws

and work on them.

What good
is anything

if you don't see past
the obvious.

If you overlook
what it is

that brings you
peace.

What good
are all these things

if you wake up
every morning pretending

to be
someone

you're not.

If you're not willing
to let go

of all these things
that bring you down.

It's hard
to find yourself

in an ocean
of people.

It's hard to listen
to your own voice

when all you hear
is noise.

It's hard
and as time goes on

it gets
even harder.

But this I preach.
This I live by.

This
I cannot

let go of—I
refuse to.

You have to love yourself
day in and day out.

Accept yourself,
forgive yourself...

work on yourself.

And it's not something
that'll happen overnight.

It's not something
you can buy

or something
you can find.

No.

It's something that takes
work... days,

weeks, years
and sometimes

even an entire lifetime.

Self-love
is a process

and sometimes
you'll fall out of it

but almost always
do you find

your way back.

Inhale this
with all lungs.

With all honesty
and all fire

in your soul.

Self-love
is a blessing,

an opportunity to find
happiness

in all places
and all things

you never thought
you would.

OLDER I GET

The older I get
the more I value

myself
and what I do

with my time.

You just know
when to let go

and when
to hold on.

When to isolate yourself
to reflect

and when to surround
yourself

with those
you need

the most.

ONLY WITH THOSE

There's no reason
for you

to be sad
at such a young age.

You have
your entire life

in front of you.

Don't let someone
who doesn't love you

close your heart.

There are so many reasons
to smile

and so many reasons
to share

that beautiful heart
of yours...

but only
with those

who deserve it
most.

Let that be
the holy word.

WISH IT UPON YOU

They see you minding
your own business.

They see you trying
to move ahead.

Trying to do
all that you can

to survive.

And still,
some people want

to destroy you.

They want
to put you down

without knowing
who you are.

Without understanding
what you've been through

or knowing
what's in your heart.

Some people,
I swear,

only want to see
you fall.

Only want to applaud
your failures

and slowly
stick knives

through your back.

Know the difference
between friend

and foe.

Know the difference
between deep love

and cheap lust.

Know the difference
between who you want

and who you need.

It could all
go so far

if only
you learn the difference.

If only
you learn

how to separate
the two.

Keep your distance.
Know your surroundings.

And let the people
who want to love you…

love you.

And those who don't,
well,

just let them be.

You should never wish
bad things

on anyone
including those

who wish it
upon you.

ON THE WAY

Stop dwelling
on the past.

They don't deserve you.

They don't deserve you
at your best

or your worst.

So stay focused.
Stay away from drama.

And stay patient...
someone worth your time

is on
the way.

BEAUTIFUL THAN BEFORE

I don't know why
we are the

way we are.

Why we hold on
to people

who are no longer here.

Why we hold on
to the past

and why we let
our memories

influence our future.

I don't know many things,
therefore,

I don't know why
so many people

come to me
for answers—for

advice.

For some kind
of revelation,

something, anything,
to give them

what they need
to let go.

To give them
what they need

to move on.

To give them the courage
to take the risk

they desperately need.

But I get it,
it is all too human

to feel lost.

To feel insignificant.
To feel as if

you're broken...
no matter how good

your life is.

It is almost human,
too human

to feel disconnected.

To want to isolate yourself
the moment

things aren't going your way.

I don't have
all the answers to all

of these questions
I am asked.

Hell,
I barely have enough
to make sense of my own

but I will say this
out loud.

I will share this
with the world.

The human heart
forgives

and it does so
under any circumstances.

Under any form
of government

or religion.

People are looking for peace.
People are looking for love.

And people
are ultimately looking

for freedom
and happiness

no matter what stage
they are in—in

their lives.

Like I said,
I don't know why

we are
the way we

are but I am certain
about one thing.

People are always searching
for more.
They're always looking

for ways to better
themselves,

no matter who notices
and who doesn't.

People,
above all,

want some kind of reassurance
that everything

will turn out okay.

So if you're looking
for a sign

then this is it.

Understand
that today

is a good day,
and it is also

a good time
to let everything that hurts

go.

Moving on

has never felt
more beautiful

than before.

But what would I know,
I am just

another writer in search
for more.

HURT US AGAIN

*I just want
to fall in love*

*with you
over and over*

again.

*And hold you
until nothing*

*can hurt us
again.*

LITERALLY EVERYTHING

Pay attention
to the way people act

when you're not
doing well.

Pay attention
to who reaches out

and who defends you

when you
need it most.

Pay attention
to who's constantly concern
with your well-being

and who genuinely
wants

what's best for you
and who doesn't.

Pay close attention,
that's all.

Knowing the difference

between who you deserve
and who you don't...

is literally
everything.

SAME ORDEAL

You're trying to better
yourself—trying

to move on.

So there's no reason
for you

to keep bringing up
your past.

No reason
for you

to keep dwelling
in what

you're trying to grow from—grow
out of.

If you're trying
to get over someone,

then you must learn
how to loosen up your grip

a little.

You must learn
how to let people go

and you must learn
how to never put yourself

in that
same situation again.

You win some,
you lose some

but if you go through
the same ordeal

twice

then you've learned
nothing

at all.

FACTS

Sometimes
people need their space.

That's all.

THE NEED TO GO

I want you
and I don't want you

to let go
of me

over something
so small.

Let me make things right.

Let me work
on my insecurities

and show you
how good relationships

don't just happen overnight.

Through hard times
or not...

I don't want to lose you
to realize

how much
I need you—how

much I love you...
because I am here for good,

and hope to God
he gets us

to where we belong.

I pray
he keeps us together,

no matter what
kind of bullshit

life has in store for us.

I hope
we don't drift apart.

MORE UNITY

I don't like
repeating myself

but there's something
I have to get off

my chest.

Something
that's been beating

at me.

Something
I'm trying to make peace

with.

And it's heavy.

And it makes me feel
like I am drowning.

Like
I am falling backwards,

then upwards
toward the sky.

If I am doomed
and if my soul

is slowly being swallowed
by the darkness

then I want you
to know

that I've been trying
to get a hold

of my life back.

I've been trying
not to fall

into the lies.

The space
that never fills

the void in my heart.

I don't believe
in the fallacies.

I don't believe
in their fake love.

Their lust for flesh

and lust for money.

I don't want
any part of it,

I'm sorry.

I've had enough.

My brothers
and sisters.

I just want peace
of mind.

I just want
to love freely

without discrimination.

I just want
my soul to expand

across the universe
and hug it

until it becomes one
with the stars.

Until the black holes
release the light

we need to see
what matters.

*The real issues,
you know?*

The real things
that make us human.

I don't need
more war.

*I need
more love.*

I don't need
more vaccines.

*I need
better foods*

that support life.

I don't need
more judgment.

*I need
more unity—more*

*understanding—more
sympathy.*

And I don't need
your science

when all I need
is faith—drive,

inspiration
something

to lean on.

Something
to believe in

even if it's *not*
physically here.

I don't like repeating myself
but I want

to help people.

I just don't have
the slightest clue

on how to start.

NOT WITH ME

I don't want
to see you in pain

and I don't want
you to go through

what I'm currently
going through

without you.

Even if
we're not together

I want to see you
do good.

I want to see you
happy.

I don't care
about the social commentaries

or the social cues.

I don't care
if we're not supposed to

speak again.

I want to see you smile,
even if

it's not with me.

I want you
to love yourself

*before you give
the universe within*

you

to someone else.

DAMN.

You lost her
and it wasn't because

you didn't love her.

It was because
you didn't communicate

with her.

You didn't pay attention
to her.

You didn't show her
affection

and you didn't take the time
to understand

what she was feeling.

You lost her
and you didn't have

to break her heart
to convince her

to move on.

THE RIGHT PLACE

I'm so very sorry
for all the terrible things

you've been through.

I'm so very sorry
for your pain—for

the chaos
that keeps you up

at night.

Your heart is loud
and it requires

a lot of attention.

A lot of time
and a lot of patience.

A lot of sunlight
and water to grow.

I'm so
very sorry

for your past.

I know
it has convinced your heart

that you're not worthy
of love.

That you're not capable
of giving it

or

of taking it
in return.

I'm so
very sorry

for all you've endured.

From the people
who've taken you for granted.

To the ones
who've made you feel

more alone.

I am sorry
for all they've caused

you.

I am sorry.
I am sorry.

I am...
so very sorry.

But let me say
this to you

with my soul exposed.

Let me be the first
to say

that you're *not* broken.

That you're not
some fucked up human being.

That you're *not*
your doubts

and you're *not*
what they've been telling you

for all
these years.

Yes,
you've been through hell

but that doesn't mean
you've got to live

in the fire,
baby.

That doesn't mean
you've got to make sense

of your past
all at once.

Sometimes
bad things

are going to happen
and sometimes

you aren't supposed
to know why.

Sometimes
you just have to trust

what God has planned
for you

no matter how tragic
life gets.

No matter what you lose

or what you sacrifice.

Timing is everything.
Perspective is important

and whether or not

you find the lesson
in what hurts...

is completely
up to you.

Just keep your heart
in the right place

and never settle
for less.

HOLD ME

*I just want you
to love me*

*a little harder
when I feel*

*like I'm breaking
apart.*

AND THEN

And then
you wonder

if love is for you.

And if it is real
and if it is something

you deserve.

Sweet love,
it is not that love

doesn't exist
and it is not

that you
do not deserve it

because you do.

It is just...
you have given your heart

to the wrong people
and I am sorry

you have given them

your all
and have received

nothing in return.

*Some people
are assholes.*

*There's no better way
to define them*

other

than that.

DO IT YOURSELF

I'm sorry
they've hurt you

the way
they've hurt you

but my heart
is not

a rehabilitation center.

My soul
cannot mend wounds.

I love you
for who you are,
as you are

but I cannot fix you
or heal you.

That is something
only you

can do

for yourself.

PEOPLE YOU LOVE

Stop asking
the people you love

how
they're doing.

Start asking them
how they're feeling.

If they feel empowered.
If they feel inspired.

Start asking them
if they're feeling well.

If they feel exhausted.

If they feel safe
or stressed.

Ask them about
their well-being.

Get into it.

Ask in detail
because when you ask

how they're doing
most of the time

they'll respond they're okay...
when they're really

not.

It's not easy
opening up

but if you ask
the right questions

then the right answers
will follow.

And be patient
with them

and never give up on
the people

you love.

LOVE YOURSELF

I'm glad to see you
doing well.

I'm glad
that after everything

you've been through,
you found a way

to smile again.

I drink to this.

To see you happy.

To see you strive
for greatness.

To see you fight
for your dreams

and what you believe in.

I write to this.

Celebrate this.

To know that it is possible

to find yourself again.

That it is possible
to find the light

when all you see
is darkness.

I'm happy for you
and as your friend,

watching you heal
has inspired me

again.

It has made me realize
how important it is

to let go.

How important it is
to forgive.

How important it is
to love yourself

no matter how dark
it gets.

I'm glad to see you

doing well,
I really am

and I just want you to know
that the next time

your world seems
to be

falling apart.

I will be with you
no matter what.

I will never leave
your side.

Till death do us part.

I love you,
my friend

and I will continue
to wish the best

for you...
always

and at all cost.

WITHOUT YOU

Sometimes
I look at you

and think:

"I hope
I never lose you."

Because

I can't help
but to wonder

if I could survive
in this world

without you.

You mean that much.

COME WITH TIME

It takes years to learn
the difference

between who
to let go

and who
to be patient with.

The same way
it takes years

to know
what you deserve

and what you don't.

Hang in there,
growth

and experience
come with time.

ANYTHING YOU DO

You find the strength
you need

at the right moment.

The same way
you find the right people,

too.

So be patient
with your timing,

trust
your process

and cut people off
when you feel

the need to.

Just make sure
not to close your heart

for anyone
and make sure

you put your soul

into
anything you do.

There is no
one path

to your greatness.

BEST FOR YOU

When you're
in a toxic relationship

you can't hate
your friends

when they don't
agree with it

or support it.

Your friends
want to see you fly,

not drown.

They want to see you
at peace,

not lost in chaos
and they definitely

want to see you
surrounded by laughter,

not covered
in tears.

So pay attention
to them.

Put the effort
to do so,

they're on your side
and sometimes

they know you
better than you know

yourself.

And clearly,
sometimes they know

what you deserve.

They only want
what's best for you,

that's all.

INTERFERE

It's okay
to love hard

but it's not okay
to think that the person

you love
is someone

you have to control
or silence

just to get
your point across.

It's not okay
to treat them

like you own them
and it's not okay

to think
they have no say

in anything.

People have this tendency
to be with someone

and believe...

that love
is making decisions

for them.

That love
is telling them

what they should be
doing—what

they should be
thinking

and feeling.

Well,
that's not it

and if you think it is...

then

you have a lot
of growing up to do—a lot

of reflecting to do
because love

isn't putting barriers
on people.

It isn't caging someone
because you're afraid

to lose them.

Because you're afraid
they might find

someone better.

Love is kind,
my friend.

You don't take a bird
and clip their wings.

You gently hold them
with open arms

and let them soar
and if they come back,

then they're yours
and if they don't...

then they were never
meant to claim

as your own.

You have to love people
for who they are

and not interfere
with who they want

to be.
That is the truth.

Just let them be.

All else,
will figure itself out.

IN THE WORLD

It may cost you
your heart

to cut
someone off

but it will cost you
nothing to grow

and learn
from the experience.

Let go,
it's okay.

Elevation
sometimes requires

isolation
and know,

how sometimes
giving yourself the time

you need

is one
of the most

humbling things
in the world.

It's liberating.

Feel the freedom.

Inhale it.
Live by it.

*It could all still be
so very beautiful.*

HARMFUL

It's sad
how people would rather

cut you off
instead

of apologize to you.

How people
would rather

ignore their flaws
but point the finger

at you
when you're wrong.

It's sad,
it really is.

Some people
never mature

and some people
never own up

to all the harm
they've caused.

PEOPLE HAVE IT

You have everything
you need.

Sure,
right now

you feel
a little empty,

a little broken
but you won't feel

like that
forever.

Count your blessings.

So many people
have it worse.

Someone,
somewhere, is wishing

they have
what you have.

PAY ATTENTION

This is your life
in a moment

and you don't have to break
someone's heart

to lose them.

Pay attention to those
you love.

Show them you care.

Give them
the attention they need.

Let them know
how important

they are to you.

Communication is everything
when you're in love

and letting them know
how you feel

is the best way

to ensure
that they'll stay.

So keep your heart open,
share it carefully

and remember,
be patient

with yourself
and the people

you love.

Live by this.
Love by this.

Now go on
and express yourself

the way you were
meant to.

IN THE WAY

I promise
to be mature

and handle our differences
with care.

I promise
to listen to you

and to treat you
with respect

and not *fuck*
with your heart.

Because it's not so hard
to do—to

put in the effort
to make it work.

So if something
is bothering you

then I'm going
to help you fix it.

Because I care,

goddamn it,
and I know you

have a long list
of people

who've done you wrong
but I vow

to be there for you.

You deserve someone
who can light up your soul.

Someone
who's not going to

destroy
what you think about love

but someone
who's willing to repair it.

And make you forget
your past.

You deserve it
and I deserve it,

too, despite

everything
we've been through.

Let's not let
our insecurities

get in the way.

WHAT I WANT

How do you expect me
to understand you,

when you get angry
every time you ask

for my opinion.

Let's be adults.

We can agree
to disagree.

We can open our hearts
and not have to

worry
about shame

or disencouragement.

I want to understand you.

I don't want
to fight you.

I want to know
why you feel

the way you feel

and I want it
to bring us closer together.

Not drift us
further apart.

Because with me
you don't have to be

so sensitive
all the time.

You can put your guard down.

I'm not here
to get you.

I'm not here
to bury you beneath

your pain
and sorrow.

I'm here for you
and *only* you.

So please,
let me talk to you.

Let me hold you
and walk with you.

I want to get
to know you

for who you are.

I am caught in your web.

Please
don't let me slip away.

THE WORK IN

Age doesn't mean
anything.

You can be
30 years old

and still
not have your life

in order
or you can be

16
and know exactly
what you want

to do.

Maturity has no limits

and you can do
anything you wish...

as long
as you believe

and put the work in.

I BELIEVE

At first,
of course,

everything will be perfect.

You will even believe
you found

the one.

But let some time pass.

Let them get out
of their comfort zone.

Let them break out
of their shell.

Some people
are going to treat you

the way
they want to treat you.

So give it
a few months.

Let their actions speak

over their words
and pay close attention

to the way
some of them change.

Because like the old saying goes.

*"How they treat you
is how they feel about you."*

And I'm a firm believer
in that.

WHAT WE WANT

In the end,
it's just me

and the people I love.

The ones
who never gave up

and the ones
who are still here.

ASK YOURSELF

Are you in love
or are you just comfortable

or afraid
to leave?

Ask yourself this question.

Answer it.

What's holding you together?
Why are you still there?

Is it security?
Is it hope?

Is it believing
that one day

they'll change?

Ask yourself
how long can you hold it in?

How much
do you think

you can take?

The world is dark,
yes it is,

but you staying with someone
you don't love

makes it
even darker,

it makes it
even colder—too

cold to sustain
life itself.

So ask yourself
if you're happy.

Ask yourself
if this is whom you want

to spend the rest
of your life with

because forever
is a long time

to live in a place
you don't call

home.

And it's sad to write
or say,

I know.

And you might even feel
terrible about it

but if you don't love them
then let him go.

Let him find
someone he deserves

and let yourself find
someone, too.

Someone
who's on the same page

as you.

So please,
let it go.

It's been a good run
but it's time to move on.

Staying any longer
could possibly destroy you

and him.
And believe me,

that's the last thing
you want to do.

Staying with someone
you don't love.

Spending any more time
with someone you don't

want.

Imagine that,
your whole life

being dedicated to something
you don't like.

There is nothing worse
than that.

You both
deserve more.

ONE YOU LOVE

If you love her
you'll change for her

and vice versa.

It's not supposed
to be easy.

You always
have to sacrifice

something

for the one
you love.

REALLY FEELS

You take her
to these expensive dinners.

You buy her
all of these

useless gifts
she doesn't need.

You give
and you give

and you give
but you give

all the wrong things.

And it's funny
because

what she really wants
from you

is priceless
and sadly,

you're too damn busy
to notice

how alone
she really feels.

GIVE IT TO YOURSELF

People don't change
for other people.

They change
for themselves.

So if they keep doing
you wrong,

then don't feel too bad
for cutting them out

of your life.

Don't feel too bad
for letting them go.

You should never regret
putting yourself first—loving

yourself first.

You deserve to,
and if

no one
is willing to love you,

then
by all means,

you deserve
 to give it

to yourself.

Self-love
is a beautiful thing.

WHO I WAS

Young man,
you want to let her go,

I understand
but the sad part is,

she actually cares
about you

and your well-being.

She actually wants
to see you grow,

to see
the both of you grow

together.

You don't let a girl
like that go.

A girl
who prays for you.

Who loves you
with her soul.

You live
in her heart, man

but you're too busy
to even notice it.

You're too into yourself
and your friends

to even begin
to appreciate her worth.

Like I said,
her heart is your home

but you're too careless
to close the door

and make it
your own.

And the worst part is,
how one day,

maybe ten years down the line
or maybe even less.

You'll be somewhere
with your comrades

and they will be

with their wives
and maybe

you'll be alone
or maybe

you won't
but that doesn't matter.

Nothing does.

Because you'll think about her
and you'll wish

you had
a second chance

to make things right.

But she will be
with someone she deserves

and it will be
too late.

This is when
your soul breaks

and this is how
it happens

all the time.

The moment you finally
realize

you've lost her.

The only woman
who wanted you

in her heart.

The only woman
who gave a damn.

I SHOULD LOVE MYSELF

I'll never abandon you.

I don't leave people,
it's not in my nature

to do so.

I work through it.
I find a solution.

I fight
and fight

until the end.

That's how much
I care,

and somehow,
some people

still find it within themselves
to leave.

I love
and I do

so deeply

but I have come to the conclusion
that no one

can love me
more

than I could
love myself.

That is
the raw truth.

Feel this in your soul.
Believe it.

Never isolate yourself
from this.

Love yourself.

Too much or
too little.

Love yourself
before it is

too late.

TOO GREAT

It's not that complicated.

If they love you,
they'll wait for you.

No matter how much
time passes.

If they love you
they'll wait

a lifetime
till you're ready.

I suppose,
time and love

is all we need.

SUNLIGHT

I'm sorry,
I don't have time

to hate you
or dwell

in our past.

I'm too busy
watering my own flowers

and making sure
they get

enough sunlight
to grow.

NEVER ASSUME

Never assume
you know someone

by what you've heard.

People like
to twist things up

and not always
in a bad way

but also,
in not a very good way

neither.

You don't know
someone's story

until you've sat with them.

Until they've opened up
to you.

Don't assume anything.

Everyone has their own
story

and everyone has their own
way of expressing it.

All you have to do
is listen.

So remember,
when it's your time

to speak…

never say more
than what they need

to know.

And never say more
than what you're

willing to lose.

WALKING AROUND

You can't feel
too bad

for someone
who constantly talks

about
their *shit* situation

but does nothing
to get out of it.

The same way
you can't help them,

if they're not willing
to help

themselves.

THE BEST THING EVER

Because
you're not broken.

You're not lost
and you're not empty.

The thing is,
everyone gets broken down

sometimes
by people

who barely understand
themselves.

By people
who are not sensitive

or kind.

By people
who don't have

the slightest clue
on what it's like

to walk
in your shoes.

So how could you think
you're weak,

when every time
you fall

you come back stronger
than before.

Every time
you break,

you come back tougher...

you come back
wiser...

smarter
and holier

than before.

So keep your head up.

Keep finding it
in you

to breathe again.

You're a goddamn fighter
and fighting

for a chance to be loved
is what

you do best.

EXPERIENCE THIS

You can't let them go
and expect

to find them
in other people.

You can't find
the same love

in someone else.

That's not
how it works.

You have to let go
before you find

new love.

You have to realize
how it is

impossible to experience
the same person

twice.

Everyone you come across

will have a different
affect on you

and the way you let in
and let go

is completely up to you.

Just make sure
not to lose yourself

in the process,
and trust your heart

and intuition
when you must.

You know what's
best for you.

You can always feel the
truth in your bones.

FUNNY LITTLE GAME

It's sad
and harsh

at the same time,
because the moment

you stop
paying attention to them

is the moment
they start

paying attention to you.

Love
is a funny little game.

You chase me,
I chase you

and in the end,
we barely get

what we deserve.

NOT LOVE

You can't expect people
to be perfect.

You expect them
to live

up to your expectations.

People are going to
hurt you.

They're going to
misunderstand you.

Make you
and break you

at the same time.

It's hard to grasp,
of course it is,

but if it doesn't hurt
than it is not real.

And if they don't
have you coming back

for more
than it is not love.

Sadness is love.
Love is Sadness.

And somewhere
in-between

there is a sense of
humility.

A sense of
self-importance

and validation.

If it doesn't almost kill you
then, perhaps,

it is not love.

SO FUCKING GOOD

If I never see you again.

I just want to say,
please don't let

anyone close your heart.

Don't let
the things that bring you down

dictate
your future.

Don't let
what bothers you

overfill your mind
and don't let

the coldness
you sometimes feel

turn your heart
into stone.

The brokenness is not you.

That feeling of failure

is not you.

Before I go,
let me finish with this.

I want you
to save yourself

if it's the last thing
you do.

To find the inspiration
you need

to protect
the things you love.

To fight for them
and die for them

if you must.

And don't cry for people
who don't deserve you.

I know it is a hard thing
to do

but you must find
the will

to keep smiling
because damn,

it looks
so fucking good on you.

Goodnight.
Good-bye.

And I hope you,
find

what you think
you have lost.

ALMOST EVERYONE

Are you happy
or just comfortable?

Ask yourself.

And if your answer is
anything but love

then let them go.

They deserve better,
and so do you.

Don't let it become
a drag.

Don't just survive
but live.

Don't just be with someone
but love.

And love with all heart.

OWN LIGHT

*You're beautiful
because*

*you know your own
darkness*

*and still,
that alone*

*doesn't stop you
from finding*

your own light.

YOUR PAST

I'm sorry
for your past.

I'm sorry
for the way you've been

loved
and for the way

you haven't
been loved.

I'm sorry
for the way your heart

has turned cold.

For the way
you've become frightened

to open up.

I'm sorry you've become
like those who've hurt you.

You've become
so distant

and so very hard
to love.

I'm sorry
for everything

I truly am.

But you don't have to be
this way.

You don't have to
run away

every time someone
is interested in you.

And you don't have to create
this image of yourself

either.

It's okay to give people
a chance,

despite everything
you've been through.

It's okay
to get hurt every now
and then.

It's okay
to cry

and it's okay
to feel a little broken.

And I'm sorry
you're the way you are

but I'm not sorry
for the way you've let it

change you.

You don't have to
let a few bad relationships

make you think
you're some kind

of fucked up human being.

You don't have to
let a few heartbreaks

decide
that you're not capable

of love.

That's something

you've bestowed
on yourself.

And only you
can get yourself out of it.

I pray for you
and hope,

that maybe one day,
you'll come back to the light.

There are so many people
who are deserving

of your love.

I just hope
you don't realize this

when it is too late.

I hope you come back soon.
I hope you realize

how much more
you still have

to give.

BLIND SIGHT

You're misjudged.

They say you're not capable
of loving yourself.

That you're not capable
of being alone.

They're wrong about you.

You've loved
with the hardest

and you've isolated yourself
with the loneliest

and you've learned.
And you've felt.

And you've fallen
and gotten up.

And you've defeated
your demons

over and over again.

You're misjudged,

of course you are.

You've been through hell
and once you've been there

there's no turning back.

Once you've been there
you're fit for any type

of human relationship
and sadly,

that's something
not many

are willing to see.

BECOME YOU

You can start over.

It's not too late for you.

Know this.
Live by this.

Every morning
is a new opportunity

to change.

A new day
to become someone

you love.

God's image lives within you.

You have the ability to create.
To change. To heal.

And it is very natural to assume this.

You wake up everyday
exhaling life

from your lungs.

YOU ARE GONE

I don't understand it
and I probably never will.

But people
will take you for granted
while you're with them.

And wish
they could have you back

the moment
you're gone.

BE WITH SOMEONE

You can't be with someone
who doesn't understand

the wrong
in what they're doing.

The same way
you can't be with someone

who doesn't worry about you,
and doesn't take your feelings

into consideration
as they would their very own.

We live in a very sad world.

You shouldn't have to convince
someone

when it's time to love.

And you shouldn't have to
convince someone to stay.

Let it be known
that every day

is a good day
to love.

And let it be known
that the best kind of humans

are always the ones
who decide to stay.

THE FIRST

The first person
who breaks your heart

will teach you
three things.

1. Life goes on.
Even when you think
it won't.

Life finds a way
to go on.

So you *will* go on.

You *will* move on
and you *will* learn how to appreciate

love and life again.

It's just
a matter of time.

2. People come and go.

That's the nature of it.
The exchange of it.

You take what you learn
from them

and apply it
to the next person who finds you.

You understand
what you went through

a little more
and you never forget

the way they made you feel.

And

3. You realize what's real.

What truly matters
once they're gone.

You realize what's worth fighting for
and what isn't.

And above all,
you realize what you once thought
was the end

was really
just another beginning.

You take all the pain
and make something beautiful from it—of it.

You take all
your broken pieces

and let go
of everything

that weighs you down.

Because sorrow
doesn't last long enough
and pain

isn't meant to stay.

Choose life, forever.

Love forever, my sweet people.

No matter how many breaking points
you go through.

Live on.
Love always.

And remember,

YOU ARE NEVER ALONE.

"THE SCIENCE OF…" SERIES
IS COMING SOON - SPRING OF 2020